IMAGES
of America

DES PLAINES

They say that most of Des Plaines history occurred while waiting for a train, whether at the depot or at a railroad crossing. But the train has been central to Des Plaines, providing means for both settlers and goods to get into town and serving as a connection to Chicago. (Courtesy of the Des Plaines History Center.)

ON THE COVER: Downtown sprang up around the depot. And though the train might have brought folks downtown, they stayed for the restaurants, like the Sugar Bowl and the Zephyr Café, and to shop at Sears. This 1940s photograph of businesses on Miner Street is from the vantage point of someone waiting for a train. (Courtesy of the Des Plaines History Center.)

IMAGES
of America

DES PLAINES

David Whittingham
with the Des Plaines Public Library
and Des Plaines History Center

ARCADIA
PUBLISHING

Published by Arcadia Publishing
Charleston, South Carolina

Library of Congress Control Number: 2012940876

For all general information, please contact Arcadia Publishing:
Telephone 843-853-2070
Fax 843-853-0044
E-mail sales@arcadiapublishing.com
For customer service and orders:
Toll-Free 1-888-313-2665

Visit us on the Internet at www.arcadiapublishing.com

*This book is dedicated to Joy Matthiessen, whose hard
work preserving Des Plaines history and passion for
old photographs made this work possible.*

CONTENTS

ACKNOWLEDGMENTS

A great number of people contributed to help make this book possible, foremost the staff and volunteers of the Des Plaines History Center and the Des Plaines Public Library. Specifically at the Des Plaines History Center, thanks go to Shari Caine, Kathleen Fairbairn, Jackie Jordan, Susan Holstrom, John Burke, and the History Center's board of trustees.

At the library, thanks go to Steven Giese, Holly Sorenson, Jo Bonell, Roberta Johnson, Lynne Rubio, and John Lavalie. From the City of Des Plaines, we would like to thank Karen Kozenczak, the Des Plaines Police Department, and the Department of Public Works, as well as former associates Peggy Wetter and Nate Belonsky.

Further assistance from the community came from Rev. Dr. William Grice III and his family; Brian Wolf, a writer at Patch.com as well as a blogger for RevitalizeDesPlaines.org; Clifford Wesa; Ed Nowakowski; Jeff Delhaye; Michael Branigan, the author of *A History of Chicago's O'Hare Airport*; the McDonald's Corporation; and DesPlainesMemory.org. The staff at the Chicago History Museum was also a tremendous help.

All images are courtesy of the Des Plaines Public Library and Des Plaines History Center unless otherwise noted.

INTRODUCTION

The Des Plaines River meandered through when our story began just as it does today, but around the river, change was the constant as people arrived and the community took root and grew. Before the first settlers arrived, the area was inhabited by Native Americans of the Ojibwe, Ottawa, and Potawatomi tribes.

The earliest written records of European settlers are from the 1830s, when a cluster of small agricultural communities sprouted with the names Rand, Orchard Place, and Riverview in what later became Maine Township. In those days, the area we now call Des Plaines had a population of about 350. Chicago, the largest city in Cook County, had a population of 4,479 and was a distant 15 miles away. Soon, the old Indian trails were widened into dirt roads, allowing farmers to bring their goods to Chicago by wagon.

When the railroad was built from Chicago to Cary in 1854, it changed everything, including the town name. The first stop after the river, named Des Plaines, was where trains would stop for water from the river. A business district grew around the station near the intersection of River Road and Miner Street. In 1869, the town was first incorporated as Des Plaines. It continued to grow through the remainder of the 19th century. Settlers, mostly from Germany and England, flocked to the area to farm.

The river was at the center of it all, enticing tourists from Chicago seeking recreation. Attractions included fishing and swimming at Northwestern Park, Hiram Jefferson's excursion boat, the Methodist Campground, and saloons and bowling alleys. Visitors stayed at one of the downtown hotels, the Meyer Hotel or the Thoma House. The river also brought destruction. Frequent floods like the great one in 1881 wiped away bridges, damaged homes, and made travel impossible for weeks at a time.

Farther down the river, the village of Riverview was also growing. Several large factories were built, such as the Steel Car Works, Western Coated Paper Works, and the Schaeffer Piano Company. By 1900, the village was booming. Riverview was sometimes called Frogtown due to the racket the frogs made along the river and many creeks.

In 1900, the population of Des Plaines was 1,800. In 1915, the village declared itself dry five years prior to national Prohibition, prompting locals to refer to it as "Dry Plaines." Greenhouses became the major industry, supplying the region with fresh vegetables and flowers. After growing more than two million roses yearly, Des Plaines was also called the "City of Roses."

With World War I came intense patriotism, and all the while, the village continued to grow. Wells, paved roads, sidewalks, and the Des Plaines Theater made life much more modern. In 1925, Des Plaines became a city and annexed Riverview.

The Douglas Aircraft Plant arrived to build aircraft for World War II. It included 1,400 acres of land for factories and runways. The first C-54 Skymaster transport plane was built there in 1941. This land became O'Hare Field and later, O'Hare International Airport. After World War II, thousands of people moved to Des Plaines and the surrounding suburbs of Chicago. From 1940 to 1965, the population grew from less than 10,000 to more than 54,000.

In the 1970s and 1980s, Des Plaines had several claims to fame. In 1978, the Des Plaines Police Department led the investigation that brought serial killer John Wayne Gacy to justice. And in May 1979, Flight 191, a DC-10 leaving O'Hare, crashed into a trailer park in Des Plaines, killing 273 people, at the time the deadliest airline disaster on American soil. In 1986, the Des Plaines River severely flooded, causing damage to more than 10,000 dwellings.

Today, Des Plaines is a large and bustling suburb of Chicago. The population in 2000 was 58,720. Its proximity to O'Hare, Chicago, and major highways brings a lot of people and businesses to the area. It is ethnically and economically diverse, but as much as things have changed, some things are still the same, namely the river, which flooded again in 2011.

One
THE FIRST SETTLERS

Before there was a town there was a river, which Native Americans used for travel as well as sustenance. A number of tribes called this region home, including groups of Potawatomi, Ottawa, and Ojibwe. Many trails crossed the area and some believe a Potawatomi settlement was once situated at this bend in the river.

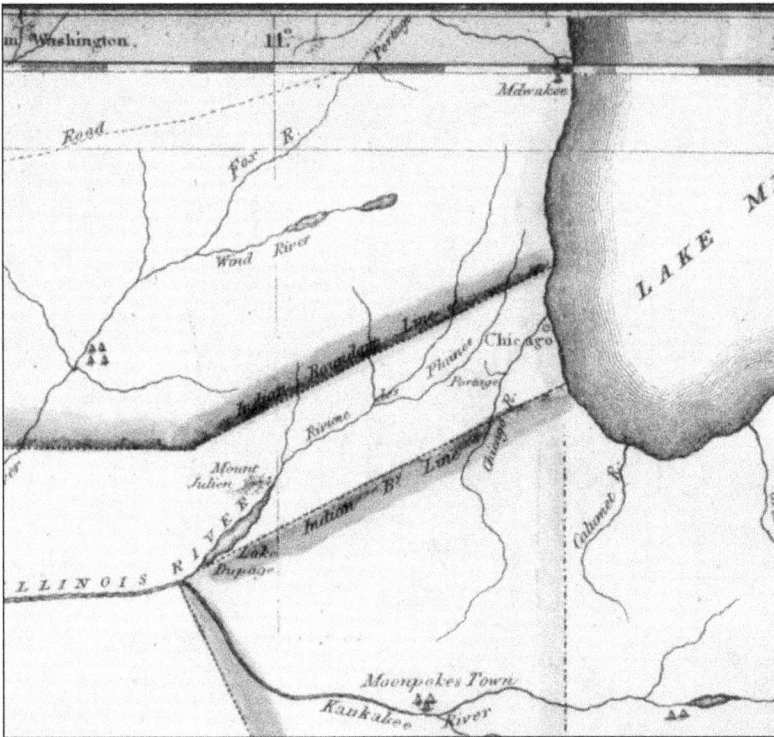

Early European explorers traveled the river, which connects with the Fox and Illinois Rivers, eventually reaching the Mississippi, and traded with the Native Americans of the region. After the Treaty of Chicago in 1833, the Potawatomi moved west, opening the area to settlers. This map was drawn by John Melish in 1818. (Courtesy of National Archives and Records Administration.)

Augustus Conant was one of the very first settlers in Des Plaines. He is seen here with his wife, Betsy Kelsey, whom he married on May 9, 1836, in what was likely the first marriage ceremony in Des Plaines. In addition to farming, he went on to become a notable preacher and temperance advocate. (Courtesy of the Chicago History Museum.)

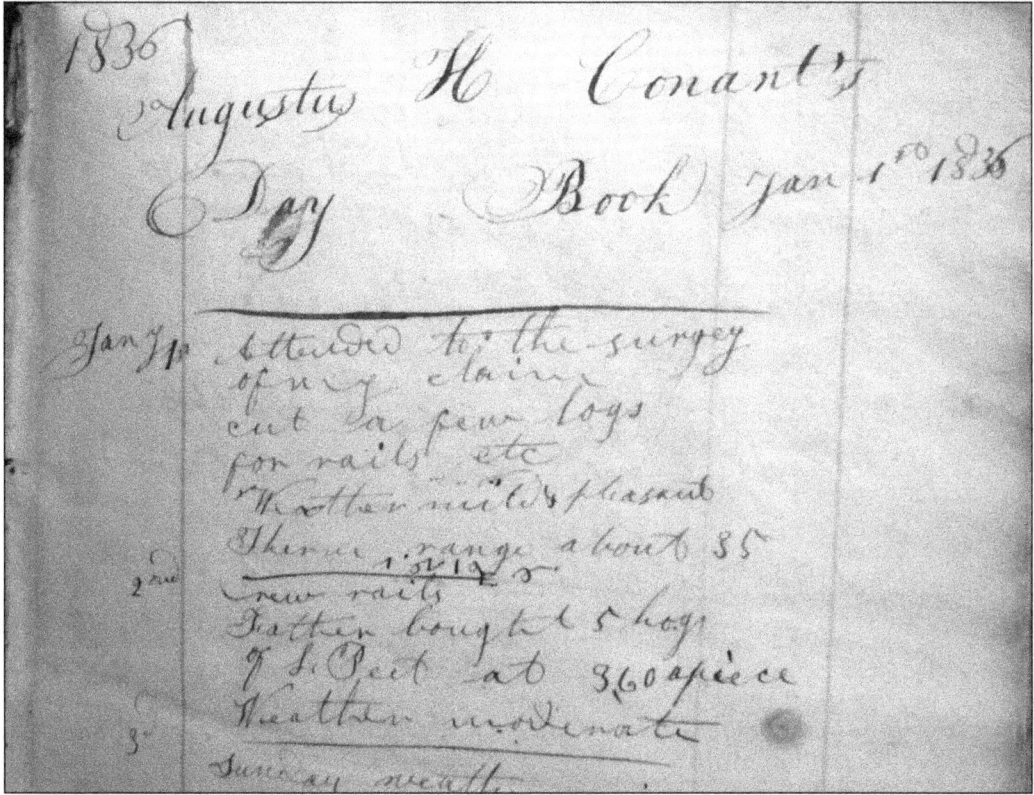

The Conant Diary, a daybook written by Augustus Conant, provides an early written record of the settler's life in the Des Plaines region. In the diary, Conant recounts the daily details and difficulties of pioneer life, beginning in 1836. It also shows the way early neighbors formed a community, helping each other through tough times. Some examples of diary entries are: "Drew rail timber across the river, evening went down to Mr. Meachem's," "helped Long raise his house," "plowed," "Went up to Mrs. Hoard's in a canoe with my wife. Read Croly's British Poets," "Killed a prairie wolf, drew wood, pumpkins oats." The diary is part of the collection of the Chicago History Museum. (Photographs by David Whittingham.)

Joseph Jefferson established a farm near what is now Oakton and River Roads. He and his sons had acquired more than $10,000 worth of property—at $1.25 per acre—by 1841. Below, working in the corn bin, are (from left to right) Edith Jefferson, the wife of Joseph Jefferson's grandson of the same name; the Jefferson sisters, May, Maude, and Emma; and their neighbor Gertie Flentge.

This wooden bridge, pictured in the 1880s, was known as the Jefferson Bridge and spanned the Des Plaines River near where Oakton Avenue runs today. At the time, bridges were considered to be temporary structures, as they were frequently damaged or destroyed in the spring floods.

Joseph Jefferson had three sons: Luther (pictured), Hiram, and Daniel. Luther built the first gristmill in the area, which was said to have been a windmill. The mill turned the Jefferson farm into a community center where neighbors came to grind their grain. By 1860, they were reportedly grinding more than 50,000 bushels of grain annually.

Socrates Rand moved to the area around 1835 with his parents, purchasing 320 acres on the west bank of the river. He became one of the most industrious and influential men of the region. In his first few years, he was elected justice of the peace, performed the first marriage (between Augustus Conant and Betsy Kelsey) in what would become Maine Township, and started the first school on his property. He was known as a road builder, plotting Rand Road in 1845, which became the major northwestern thoroughfare. The only roads in the region then were little more than trails through the wilderness. The photograph below shows River Road in the 1880s.

The Illinois & Wisconsin Railroad—later called the Chicago & North Western Railway Company—purchased land in 1852 and built a steam-operated sawmill to cut railroad ties. Socrates Rand was hired to grade the way for a future railway. This building housed the mill. Rand purchased the mill in 1855 and continued to use it as a sawmill until 1861, when it was converted into a gristmill. (Photograph by John Vacilek.)

The Rand Bridge spanned the Des Plaines River on the northern side of town. Rand Road, a former Indian trail, had become an important route, serving as a primary mail route to outlying towns.

Mancell Talcott was one of the earliest settlers in the region, building a log cabin near where Touhy Avenue crosses the Des Plaines River today. He served as postmaster from 1837 to 1840 and married Mary H. Otis in 1841. In addition to farming, he also worked with his brother Edward Benton Talcott on the Illinois & Michigan Canal and worked in both the banking and stonecutting industries. Other notable early settlers included Dr. John A. Kennicott, Dr. Silas Meacham, Elem Kinder, and Nicholas and Phineas Sherman. (Courtesy of the Chicago History Museum.)

This wooden trunk, dated from about 1864, belonged to K. Karl Schnur and is now in the Des Plaines History Center collection. Schnur was one of many settlers from Germany and the chest likely made the trek with him across the Atlantic and over land to his new home. (Photograph by Gina deConti.)

Two

A Town is Born

In 1854, the Chicago & North Western Railroad established a line from Chicago to Cary, on which Des Plaines was the third stop outside of Chicago. At that time, the small town was recorded as the "Town of Rand"—after Socrates Rand—and was a subdivision of Maine Township. Most residents then would have considered themselves residents of Maine. With the train bringing so many people to the Des Plaines station, the town followed and eventually incorporated as the Town of Des Plaines in 1869. This locomotive, known as the *Pioneer*, was built in 1837 by Baldwin Locomotive Works and was one of the first trains to run in Chicago.

The railroad brought people, both to visit and to settle. There was substantial prairie land to be farmed, and with the new train and roads into Chicago, the farmers had a way to bring their crops to market. The railroad brought tradesmen and laborers to help build the new community. In 1870, the population was close to 300.

The Chicago & North Western depot, near the Des Plaines River at the current intersection of River Road and Miner Street, allowed the trains to take on water for their steam engines. In 1859, a train set a new record, making the 91-mile trek from Chicago to Janesville, Wisconsin, in just over two and a half hours. The Des Plaines depot was reportedly the first permanent station built on the line. The water tower below was at the intersection of Ellinwood and Pearson Streets.

These two businesses, seen here in the 1860s, were among the first to pop up near the train station. The one on the left has a sign that reads "Boots Shoes & Harness Shop." The building on the right's sign reads, "Lager, Beer, Saloon, Groceries & Provisions" and was run by Christian Meinsen. These businesses were on the 1500 block of Ellinwood Street across the street from the train depot.

Just around the corner on Pearson Street, this parade was on the Fourth of July in 1893. The white building is the W.F. Meyer Store and Hotel, on Miner Street. New businesses were springing up all around the station, but the depot water tower is still seen behind the building on the left. There are even spectators on top of the water tower.

Supplies were needed to build new businesses and other buildings, so the Whitcomb Brickyard was established nearby in 1868. Above, an informal group of Whitcomb workers posed for this photograph in 1890. The brickyards (below) produced 800,000 bricks in the first year and averaged nearly three million a year thereafter. Years later, the pit where they dug their clay was turned into Shagbark Lake.

Lagerhausen Lumber was on Ellinwood Street at River Road, just east of the depot. Barney Lagerhausen sold building supplies as well as coal, flour, and feed. Above, farmers are lined up to pick up supplies. Below, a rail spur led to the west of the building, allowing for coal, lumber, and other supplies to be loaded and unloaded directly. Coal was stored in the rear building while the second floor of the front building served as a grain elevator.

Farming in greenhouses really took off in Des Plaines in the late 1800s. The greenhouses gave the farmers more control over conditions and allowed them to extend the growing season. M. Winandy and Sons was formed in 1871 and became a leading greenhouse builder in town. Above, Michael and Alfred Winandy are perched on their horse-drawn wagon. Below, the Winandy crew, with Michael, his sons Tom, Pete, Alfred, and Mike, and seven other men, build a greenhouse.

Jacob Walter opened the Walter Harness Shop on Miner Street in 1862. He passed the business on to his sons, Philip and Joseph. In his early years, Joseph drove a stagecoach carrying passengers and mail between Des Plaines and West Northfield.

Kinder Hardware is seen here in the 1870s. It opened in its original building on Miner Street between Pearson and Lee Streets around 1873. The business soon moved to the southeast corner of Ellinwood and Pearson Streets, where it sold hardware and industrial supplies for more than 100 years.

Farming was the major industry in early Des Plaines. Henry G. Koehler, seen here in his wagon, was a grower of potatoes, pickling onions, and other garden produce. Farmers would bring their crops to Chicago to sell them at market. Though only 15 miles, it was often an overnight trip.

The John Bielefeldt farm stood at the southwest corner of Oakton and Lee Streets. Here, John William Bielefeldt, Mina Bielefeldt, and Bertha Scherpels stand in front of the picket fence at the house. John's sons, William and Fred, are seated in horse-drawn vehicles, and John Meinsen holds a horse.

Johan Boeckenhauer set up his farm on Algonquin Road in 1864. Here, working with threshing equipment in the Boeckenhauer hayfield, are Johan's son (most likely one of the two men on the engine) and his grandsons William (far right) and John (standing fifth from right).

Farmers like the Kohlers, Bielefeldts, and Boeckenhauers may have bought the thresher and other farm machinery at Elwin D. Scott's farm implement store near the corner of Ellinwood and Lee Streets. The brick building to the left was later the original location of Spiegler's department store. According to a notation on the back, Elwin D. Scott is second from the left in this image.

Both locals and visitors from Chicago used the river and the woods around it for recreation, swimming, fishing, and exploring. This woman rows by a dam of stones behind the Jefferson farm. The fishing was rumored to be good here; Dana Jefferson reportedly caught a ten-and-a-half-pound pickerel at this spot in September 1891.

Hiram Jefferson operated a steam-powered excursion paddleboat on the Des Plaines River beginning in the 1870s, taking visitors up and down the river, sometimes as far north as Rand Bridge. Tour boats, like this one run by William Wille, also cruised the river.

Scene on the Des Plaines Camp Ground.

The first Methodist camp meeting was held in 1860 on land that clergymen rented near Rand's Bridge. Huge crowds arrived by train and wagon to partake in the preaching and singing. It was estimated that more than 10,000 people attended the meeting on Sunday, September 2, 1860. The permanent grounds were purchased in 1865 and the campground is still going today, making it the longest continuously running campground in the Midwest.

1859—JUBILEE—1909

Scene on the Des Plaines Camp Ground.

In the earliest years, campers slept in tents that circled an opening where religious services were held. Later, campers were able to rent tents with floors. Cabins, dining halls, a hotel, several tabernacles, and buildings that served as headquarters for missionary groups were all built. An artesian well was dug, and crystal-clear water was advertised as one of the attractions.

Dr. Clarence A. Earle (left) took over where Socrates Rand left off as the central figure in Des Plaines. After interning at Cook County Hospital, he and his wife moved to Des Plaines in 1889. He was a pioneer doctor in the truest sense, heading out in the middle of the night on horseback to tend to his patients. He lobbied for civic improvements like paved sidewalks, improved schools, and a library. He served as a medical examiner for the Chicago & North Western Railway and a number of other enterprises, and he was president of the board of education. He also pushed to preserve local history, locating the Conant Diary and later donating it to the Chicago Historical Society. His home overlooking the Des Plaines River is pictured on the postcard below.

Photo by Jones.

No. 104. Published by The Suburban Postcard Co., Des Plaines, Ill.

Looking north from New Bridge, Des Plaines, Ill.

Dr. Earle purchased his property from Socrates Rand—the land included the Rand mill building—and built the notable Earle house (above) overlooking the river at Miner Street. The Queen Anne–style house featured a distinctive dome fashioned by Kinder Hardware. The house was a symbol of Des Plaines until it was destroyed by fire in 1978.

Philippine Ahbe (1832–1927) was a well-known midwife in Des Plaines, assisting in the delivery of more than 1,000 babies and having 10 children herself. Here, she poses for a photograph with her son, John Ahbe (1872–1948). (Courtesy of Rev. Dr. William G. Grice III and family.)

William Meyer was the first Des Plaines merchant to receive a license permitting him to "keep a saloon and sell intoxicating liquors at his place of business on Miner Street in the Village of Des Plaines." The W.F. Meyer Hotel and Saloon was at Miner and Pearson Streets. (Courtesy of Rev. Dr. William G. Grice III and family.)

The Thoma House Hotel, also known as the Desplaines House, was one of the finest hotels in the area. Built in 1883 for $10,000, it featured 35 guest rooms and a well-known bar. It also had meeting rooms where the early village council meetings were held before Des Plaines had a town hall. It advertised itself as a summer resort catering to both the Methodist revivalists and those seeking recreation. Later, a bowling alley was added.

Kunisch Barber Shop, E.D. Scott's Real Estate, Held Restaurant, and Kray Jewelers were on the same stretch of Miner Street as the Thoma Hotel. Julius Kunisch established his barbershop shortly after he arrived in Des Plaines in 1884. Kray Jewelers was opened in 1893 by Ray Kray and was later run by his son, John. The company promoted itself as the timepiece inspector for the Chicago & Northwestern Railway.

Elwin Scott was a real entrepreneur. He was born in 1849 in Vermont and his family moved to the Des Plaines area in 1852. In addition to his real estate company and his farm implement business, he also ran both a popular cider mill and a printing press for the *Des Plaines News* out of this Ellinwood Street building.

Aaron Minnich operated a livery stable on Ellinwood Street in the 1870s. Later, with his son Thomas, he ran an ice business while he helped his other son, Frank, set up a saloon. The ice was cut from the Des Plaines River each winter and stored in his insulated icehouse to be sold in the warmer months. An ice cart is pictured above. The saloon (below) was later sold to Albert Fritz.

Christ Nissen operated the American House Hotel and Saloon in the 1890s in this building, which was owned by the Winkelman family. Nissen is holding the reins of the horse his son Martin is riding. The ladies' entrance led to a side parlor, as ladies could not be seen entering the saloon.

Later, the Nissen Saloon was on the west side of Lee Street just south of the railroad tracks. Visible in the front window are signs for Peter Hand Brewery, Monitor Whiskey, and a wrestling carnival.

The Curtis and Meyer store opened at 1507 Ellinwood Street in 1882. It was a grocery and general goods store that also housed one of the first post offices in town. After John H. Curtis left the business, it became the G.F. Meyer store. The second floor became the Des Plaines Hotel. Above, the driver of the store's delivery wagon gets ready to head out. Below, proprietor George Meyer oversees his storee, while Anna Hendricks Ehrlich stands behind the counter.

Mayme Flentge (left) stands with another woman at the corner of River Road and Miner Street in the 1890s. Concrete sidewalks were just being poured, an upgrade from the old wooden sidewalks. The old pumping station is in the background.

This structure was the first jail in Des Plaines. It was situated on Ellinwood Street and is seen here around 1890. It served Des Plaines until the first city hall was built, with a jail within it. This building was later used as a storage building on the Minnich property.

The first village hall was dedicated in September 1892 at the corner of Ellinwood and Lee Streets. In addition to the village offices and meeting rooms, it also housed the fire department and jail. It was even used for dances and concerts to bring in additional revenue. Below, a crew levels out the dirt before laying new gravel in front of the village hall around 1910.

Above, workers and customers stand in front of Petterson's Blacksmith Shop with horses and a carriage. Horses were an essential part of the farming community. Next door, a small sign for a meat market sticks out. Below, Edward Manuel opened E.A. Manuel Livery and Boarding Co. on Miner Street in 1895. Manuel was a licensed veterinarian, which surely helped him establish himself. His business grew through the years and eventually became United Motor Coach.

Above, one of Edward Manuel's carriages carries a group of women, possibly from the Methodist campground, on a hayride in the 1890s. Manuel holds the horse. Suburban Tea & Coffee Co. was run by J.W. Koenig on Lee Street. Below, his wagon heads out for a delivery.

Spiegler Bros. Department Store, seen here on Ellinwood Street, opened in 1900 and sold general merchandise. Many longtime residents remember going back-to-school shopping for clothes and supplies at Spiegler's.

Louis Spiegler stands on the left inside the store he founded with his brother Benjamin. Benjamin left the business in 1904, prompting Louis to change the name from Spiegler Bros. to simply Spiegler's Department Store. The store was expanded and remodeled several times over the years before moving from this location in 1977.

Kinder Hardware, run by Benjamin F. Kinder, was the longest running business in Des Plaines, operating from 1873 until it closed in 2006. It is seen here at its Ellinwood and Pearson Streets location. The image below shows the inside of Kinder Hardware around 1900. Kinder is in the center with employees William S. Longley Jr. (left) and Rudolph Kruse.

The Jefferson house is one of the oldest and most notable buildings in Des Plaines. It was built in the 1860s as part of the Jefferson farm and later became the headquarters for the Izaak Walton League, a wilderness preservation organization.

This house was built for Edward Manuel of E.A. Manuel Livery after he moved to Des Plaines in 1895. Sitting on two picturesque acres with gardens laid out by the renowned Ransom Kennicott, it was considered a jewel of the community. It remained in the Manuel family until 1991 and still stands at the corner of Rand Road and Elk Boulevard.

Benjamin Kinder and his family lived in this 1907 house at 777 Lee Street. "Lizzie" Kinder and housemaid Elsie Bosch are seen in front of the house around 1910.

The Moehling family paid $7,965 for this 200-acre farm and farmhouse in 1865. It was the last farm to close in Des Plaines, in the 1990s, but the house still stands on Rand Road near Wolf Road.

The Des Plaines River was temperamental and was known to flood. Augustus Conant made several notes of it in his daybook in the 1830s. In 1852, 13-year-old Amasa Kennicott wrote in a school essay, "[the floods] sweep away all the bridges and leave the river impassable for days, weeks altogether." The creeks that fed the river often flooded as well. The flood of 1881 was called the great flood, but it spurred the village to attempt more robust bridge construction. The Methodist campground, on the east bank of the river, was frequently under water.

Though the first schoolhouse was on the Rand property—supposedly in his cheese room—it was replaced by this two-room school building on Pearson Street in 1852. Seen here in 1868, it served the community until a new school opened in 1874. Chester Bennett was a schoolmaster at the time; his original diary is viewable at DesPlainesMemory.org.

North School opened in 1874 on River Road, just north of downtown. It served elementary students until 1952 and was torn down in 1957. In this photograph, children pose on the school steps. Playground equipment, wooden sidewalks, and a fence in the foreground are all visible.

German Lutheran School,
Des Plaines, Ill.
4329

In addition to the public schools, several schools were affiliated with local churches. For such a small community, there were a vast number of denominations accounted for, including Baptists, Catholics, Congregationalists, Episcopalians, Methodists, and Unitarians. The German Immanuel Lutheran Church and School was initially established in 1871 and convened in several buildings. After outgrowing several locations, the school above was built. It was destroyed by fire on February 4, 1918 (left). After the fire, a larger three-story building was erected in its place.

Rather than build a church, in 1885, St. Mary's Catholic Church was brought by two railcars from Arlington Heights to its location at Thacker and Cora Streets on land donated by the Gallagher family. The tiny church only held 13 pews. A new church was built in 1907 at Pearson Street and Prairie Avenue, which also included the school below.

A man and small boy pose in front of the First Christ Evangelical Church on Cora Street. It was built in 1892 and was later called Christ Church. Reverend Bloesch was the first minister and served from 1892 to 1897.

First Methodist Episcopal Church was located at Lee Street and Park Place. It was built in 1888 after their reorganization and remodeled in 1924. This building went on to house many other entities, including a youth center, an auction house, and a real estate office.

The German Evangelical Lutheran
Church on Lee Street (pictured) later
became known as the Immanuel
Lutheran Church. It was constructed
in 1876 and stood for 80 years before it
was replaced by the current building.

The Congregationalists were one of the
first denominations to organize in Des
Plaines, building their original church at
Dee and Talcott Roads. The church seen
here was located at Prairie and Graceland
Avenues and served the Congregationalists
from 1872 until 1929. It was built on
land donated by Alfred Parsons, using
bricks from Whitcomb Brickyards. The
building still stands and currently houses
the Des Plaines Masonic Lodge.

Infirmary, St. Mary's Training School,
Des Plaines, Ill
4343.

Known today as Maryville Academy, this school has been called Feehanville, St. Mary's Training School, and Maryville City of Youth. The campus, at River and Central Roads, was established by Archbishop Patrick Feehan in 1882. Starting humbly with 15 Chicago boys in a farmhouse, Maryville grew to shelter more than 30,000 children. The building above, known as "The Villa," was originally Feehan's summer home and later became an administration building. The buildings below, seen when it was known as St. Mary's Training School, have served as convent, chapel, boys' dormitory, library, and assembly hall, as well as living quarters for the brothers in charge. In 1899, the facility was damaged by a major fire, but rebuilding was completed by 1905. It first served only boys, but allowed girls in 1911.

St. Mary's Training
School, Feehanville, Ill.
25903.

Three

RIVERVIEW AND ORCHARD PLACE

Just to the south, a separate community sprang up, known as Riverview. It was also called Frogtown by some, in a reference to the loud frogs that croaked in its marshes. The boundaries were Oakton, Touhy, River, and Mt. Prospect Roads. Riverview was incorporated as a village in 1895. The Riverview Land Association planned the town to be the "manufacturing center of the northwest." It quickly became a boomtown of industry, with five factories running by 1890. Riverview's first village hall, seen here, was built in 1902.

Similar to Des Plaines, the railroad line was a catalyst, helping Riverview establish itself. In this case, it was the Wisconsin Central Railroad, later known as the Soo Line, which passed through Des Plaines and built the Riverview station in 1892. This station was near the intersection of Mannheim and Prospect Roads. Heller's Saloon was in the building just to the left of the depot.

Riverview School was built in 1893 at a cost of $1,500 at the intersection of Riverview and Illinois Streets. Below, Riverview students pose in front of their school in 1898.

With proximity to Chicago and freight and passenger train service, Riverview was primed to become a manufacturing center. It built up quickly, with at least five major factories in operation by 1900. The Columbia Steel Car Works factory is seen above, under construction in the 1890s. Columbia produced gondola freight-train cars. The Western Brass Works factory, also called Western Brass Foundry, is seen below around 1890. The Western Brass building was later converted into the Schaeffer Piano factory.

In the above image, workers in the Des Plaines Canning Company of Riverview, owned by Charles Boesche, take a break to pose for a photograph around 1900. The Western Coated Paper & Card Works (below) was located along the Wisconsin Central rail tracks near Everett Street. A 1902 fire destroyed the factory. Between 1899 and 1903, four Riverview factories were destroyed by fire; they were rumored to have been the work of a serial arsonist. After a fifth factory moved out of town, Riverview never returned to its manufacturing glory. In 1925, the town requested to be annexed to Des Plaines to share in city services.

Edward Dittman ran a general store on Prospect Avenue east of Circle Avenue in Riverview. In the 1910 photograph above, Dittman wears a jacket and cap behind the counter. The Silver Fox Farm (below) raised foxes and mink for the fur industry. Farming was also a major industry in Riverview.

The next station south on the Wisconsin Central Railroad was established for another small farming community called Orchard Place. The Orchard Place station stood on land donated by entrepreneur and real estate mogul Elwin Scott near the intersection of Higgins and Mannheim Roads in what had been the Scott family orchard. The community was eventually annexed by Des Plaines in 1956.

Peter Stellman's general store and tavern was at the center of Orchard Place. Right near the train station, it was the place to go for a meal, a drink, groceries, or a place to stay. The building on the left had a general store, a dining room, and a kitchen. The building on the right had a stable with rooms for rent. The tavern connected the two buildings.

Frank Duntemann ran Duntemann's general merchandise store and post office in Orchard Place, seen here around 1895. Located on Orchard Place Road, it was also the Duntemann family home.

The Duntemann family and their dog Rover pose for a photograph on the Meadow Creek Bridge in Orchard Place. Frank and Martha Duntemann are under the umbrella; their son Elvin is the one with the fishing pole.

Orchard Place opened its first one-room schoolhouse near Lee Street and Higgins Road in 1855. It served the small community until 1923, when a brick schoolhouse was built to replace it.

Four

A NEW CENTURY

Around 1900, Des Plaines began to transform. The small farming community would, over the course of a few decades, become a bustling suburb with all the modern amenities. This Henry McAlvey painting shows downtown as it was in 1900. It currently hangs in the Des Plaines Civic Center.

The Des Plaines station and the Chicago & North Western water tank are seen in this elevated view of downtown, taken from atop the water tower behind the village hall around 1905. Looking northeast, the Thoma House Hotel and other businesses line Miner Street behind the depot.

Ellinwood Street is visible in the bottom right corner. Behind the buildings are the homes and farms on River and Rand Roads.

#4 Bird's eye view W. DesPlaines Ill.

These bird's-eye view photographs show how the neighborhood filled in with new homes. They also show the vast expanses of farmland in the distance. Both photographs were taken from atop the water tower behind the village hall. Above, looking southwest around 1905, the near houses sit on Lee Street where it intersects Pearson Street; the 1871 Congregational Church is seen as well. The view below is northwesterly around 1915. Some notable buildings include the Simeon Lee home (bottom left), for whom Lee Street is named, and the Nissen Saloon (bottom right). Miner Street runs in the background with the original Des Plaines Public Library and the Kelso house behind.

#5 Birds-eye view N.W. Des Plaines, Ill.

After Pres. William McKinley was assassinated in September 1901, the country mourned. Village Hall (right) was dressed with flags and bunting in his honor. Des Plaines residents were a patriotic group; dozens of photographs remain from early parades, such as the one below, from the Fourth of July in 1909. The two men display early firefighting equipment. Behren's store, on the far left, is festively decorated for the event.

The Des Plaines Bandstand was just north of downtown, at Lee Street and Park Place. It was built in 1892 and featured a six-foot-high stage for open-air concerts. On many nights, residents would come out for the music and enjoy an ice cream on the lawn. The Des Plaines Military Band (below) played the bandstand on most Thursdays in the warmer months as well as for special events and holidays. Harry Bennett, the last Des Plaines village president, was bandmaster for a time.

The pumping station was one of Des Plaines's more recognizable buildings. Just south of downtown on River Road, it was built in 1908 to shelter the pumping equipment for the village's artesian well, which was completed in 1903.

Many of the photographs of early Des Plaines were taken by William Thiede, seen here with village president Fred Brasel outside his Lee Street studio.

The first Des Plaines Public Library opened in 1907. It was initially funded by a $5,000 grant from Andrew Carnegie. The funds were procured due to the tireless efforts of Dr. Clarence Earle, whose first grant request had been rejected. The village approved hiring Sarah Weeks as the first librarian at a salary of $10 a month.

Many members of the community supported the new library and other civic endeavors. Elwin D. Scott is seen here in his Scott Real Estate Office in 1902. He gave the first donation—$10—to the library in 1904. In the 1880s, he spurred the development of the Wisconsin Central Railroad (later the Soo Line) through Des Plaines and Orchard Place by donating land for the Orchard Place station.

70

Dr. Earle was a major catalyst in establishing Maine Township High School. It was built on Thacker Street near Ashland Avenue in 1902. It was initially designed to serve 250 students, but was later expanded to hold up to 650. The greenhouses in front were part of Charles F. Arnold's florist business, which was located at 1539 Thacker Street.

Since the population was outgrowing North School, South School was built in 1906 on the corner of Thacker and Lee Streets. It was later renamed Central School.

Through everything, the river continued its destructive ways. Spring floods were common, but the 1910 flood seen above was particularly bad. And with the still unpaved roads under water, travel was impossible for days. Northwestern Park and the Methodist campground were frequently submerged as well.

Above, Des Plaines volunteer firemen pose with a 1920s fire truck parked in front of the village hall. Some of the men are, in no particular order, police chief Dick Hammer, fire chief Axel Petterson, Ed "Tack" Nagel, Mr. Hintz, George Kinder, Mr. Lueck, John Hammerl, and Nick Geisen. Riverview police officer Willie Duntemann is seen at right with his motorcycle around 1910. Des Plaines got its first motorcycle policeman in 1922.

Though the kids above are just fooling around, the smashed automobile shows that emergency personnel were indeed needed. With so many railroad crossings, there were a lot of accidents between trains, cars, and pedestrians on both the Chicago & North Western line and the Wisconsin Central Railroad/Soo Line. Below, onlookers view the wreckage of a train collision on the Wisconsin Central line in 1901.

A REAR END COLLISION
ON WISCONSIN CENTRAL RY
AT DESPLAINES ILL JUNE 13 1901
PHOTO BY J.R. STELLMAN

Crossing guards were set up at the busy intersections with flares to prevent collisions. The crossing guard for Lee Street downtown is seen above, and the Pearson Street crossing guard is below. In 1919, the Illinois highway commissioner threatened to fine the Soo Line $100 a day if it did not install auto-stops or employ 24-hour crossing guards.

Despite occasional accidents, the railroad was still essential, perhaps even more than before. By this time, instead of occasional trips to Chicago, some residents had become regular commuters. Traveling to downtown Chicago was fast, easy, and relatively inexpensive.

The Des Plaines depot was replaced in 1914. The old depot, which had served the community since the 1850s, was moved a block west where it was used as a storage facility. The new depot was larger and featured concrete platforms, electric lighting, and spacious waiting rooms.

Edward Manuel, known for his horse livery service, successfully transitioned into the new automotive age with the establishment of Suburban Auto Livery and later the United Motor Coach bus company. Many students depended on the bus service to get to Maine Township High School.

This Stanley Steamer is thought to have been the first automobile owned in Des Plaines. Above, Philip and Annette Parsons take a road trip in the Steamer in Iowa around 1909. Below, riding with the top down, are Elmer Wicke (far left), who served as village president from 1915 to 1923, and Charles Hammerl (second from left), who was mayor from 1929 to 1933.

The introduction of the automobile transformed Des Plaines. Miner Street is already flooded with cars in the 1915 photograph above. Some of the businesses are the *Des Plaines Suburban Times*, First National Bank, and the Great Atlantic and Pacific Tea Company (A&P) grocery. The photograph above was taken from the same vantage point as the photograph on the cover of this book, but about 30 years earlier. Below, businesses like Minnich's Ice no longer needed to deliver their goods by horse and buggy, improving efficiency.

Gas stations sprang up to fill the need for fuel. The Standard Oil station above was at the corner of Des Plaines Avenue (River Road) and Miner Street. Richard Landmeier was the attendant during the late 1920s and early 1930s. Car dealerships appeared around that time as well, and businesses adapted to the new way of doing things: Edward Manuel sold Hupmobiles and Dodge Brothers automobiles out of his livery on Miner Street and the Poyers ran the tire, battery, and radio shop pictured below.

Lawn tennis and other yard games like croquet were popular. The partygoers above sit for the camera at an event at the Parsons home at Lee and Prairie Streets. Below, campers at the Methodist campground enjoy a game of croquet.

"Croquet"
M.E. Camp Grounds.
Des Plaines, Ill.
74

The Echo Theatre was Des Plaines's first movie house, opening around 1915. On Lee Street just south of Ellinwood Street, it featured vaudeville shows and silent movies. In 1916, it advertised that it showed "nothing but clean, censored movies," which cost just a nickel.

Gilbert and Sullivan's *The Mikado* was performed at the Echo Theatre in 1915. The show was put on by the Des Plaines Commercial Association to raise money for new street signs in the village. The cast was made up of many prominent citizens along with members of the Congregational Church choir. It was directed by Pansy L. Talcott; Harry T. Bennett served as the music director.

The Married Men's Baseball Team, seen here around 1904, was one of a number of baseball teams playing at the time. Games like this were played to benefit various causes, like this game in Stars Park, which raised money for the forthcoming Des Plaines Public Library.

Northwestern Park was on the east side of the river next to the Methodist campground. The park was initially on land owned by the Benjamin Poyer family; he allowed groups to hold picnics on his property. After it became a public park, it added a refreshment stand and a dance pavilion. Art Minnich (below) was a well-known tuba player, and his band, the Hungry Five, garnered some attention. Minnich was also an anchoring member of the Chicago & North Western Railway Band.

Above, the Progressive Federation Band played at the Northwestern Park Labor Day picnic in 1914; below, the Herman Kruse Orchestra featured Alvin Minnich on drums. Some other bands that played in Des Plaines were Millar's Orchestra, the Dreamland Jazz Band, and Les Fulle's Band.

The Clown Band was an offshoot of the Chicago & North Western Railway Band. They made people laugh and developed quite a following. The railroad formed the band to promote harmony with the public and among its employees.

Five

FROM WORLD WAR I THROUGH WORLD WAR II

Des Plaines got swept up in the patriotism surrounding World War I. Residents were encouraged to display the flag, and parades and marches were common. Hundreds of Des Plaines men served in the war. These men march behind several soldiers down Miner Street in 1917, likely on their way to camp.

BELLEAU WOODS - FOREST PRESERVE
DES PLAINES, ILL.

The Forest Preserve system was established in 1919. Seeing the importance of preserving native woodlands and saving threatened local species, Dr. Clarence Earle advocated for the creation of forest preserves as early as 1910. Most of the land surrounding the river in Des Plaines, including Northwestern Park, is part of the Forest Preserve system. In 1923, a monument dedicated to troops killed in World War I was put up in Belleau Woods.

DESPLAINES RIVER - FOREST PRESERVE
DES PLAINES, ILL.

Around 1919, several dams were put in the Des Plaines River to raise the water level. Here, Dam Number Two was built with a concrete ledge that cars could drive across if the water was not too high. It featured a wooden footbridge for pedestrians to cross as well as a swimming area and even a large slide at one point. It was a popular spot for carnivals and picnics.

Pageants and fashion were big during the "Roaring Twenties." In 1924, Savena (Ahbe) Gorsline was honored as Miss Des Plaines. She went on to become Miss Illinois in 1928 and came in third in the Miss USA pageant. She even composed the song, "You Will Like Des Plaines," which was played to promote the city.

Even with all of these games, concerts, and pageants, there was a very moral and pious element in the Des Plaines community. In fact, Maine Township voted itself dry in 1914, five years before nationwide Prohibition (under the 1919 Volstead Act) went into effect. Imig's Saloon became Imig's Ice Cream Parlor and the town adapted, soon giving itself the nickname "Dry Plaines."

There were still ways to get alcohol during the dry years. Roger Touhy and his brothers bootlegged liquor in the northwest suburbs. Touhy had ties to organized crime and was both a supplier and a rival to Al Capone. In 1934, he was sent to prison for 20 years on a trumped-up kidnapping charge that a judge later declared a hoax. Touhy (third from left) is seen here in the courtroom. (Courtesy of the Chicago History Museum.)

In the 1920s, the downtown area went through a revitalization and the new buildings grew to define the community. The Des Plaines Theater (above) was built by the Polka brothers in 1925 on the corner of Miner and Lee Streets. The elaborate theater was the pride of the northwest suburbs for its first few years. It showed movies all week and had a special five-act vaudeville show on Sundays. Gene Autry even performed there in 1935. The Masonic Temple (below) across the street was also erected in 1924. The building, with its large auditorium, has long been a community center. Some notable tenants were the Sixteen Screen, the Lyric School of Music and Dancing, the Army Reserve Youth Group, the Des Plaines Church of Christ, and the Des Plaines Theater Guild.

First National Bank, Des Plaines, Ill. 12621

Many other new and notable buildings were appearing downtown. The Des Plaines State Bank (above) was built around 1927 next to the Echo Theatre. It was elegant, with a Georgia marble exterior and classically influenced architecture. The Des Plaines State Bank did not make it through the Great Depression, but in the years after, the building housed several other banking institutions as well as the Des Plaines Public Library in 1936 and 1937, while the new library was being built. Another classically influenced building, the original First National Bank building (right) on Miner Street was built in 1913 and still stands today. The First National Bank operated there until it moved into the Des Plaines State Bank building in 1937.

The greenhouse industry thrived in Des Plaines, with a number of companies supplying Chicago with freshly cut flowers. Greenhouse growers at the time included Hoefle and Sons (above and below), the Garland Brothers, Bauske, Blewitt, and Standke.

Des Plaines grew millions of hothouse roses annually, earning it the moniker "City of Roses." Premier Rose Gardens was the largest rose producer in the area at the time.

Fred Pesche is the proprietor of Pesche's Flowers, located on River Road. It is one of the few greenhouses remaining from the City of Roses era. Over the years, it has also sold wine and foods as well as flowers, and it is still going strong today. (Courtesy of Pesche's Flowers.)

President Roosevelt's Works Projects Administration (WPA) was involved in several Des Plaines building projects in the 1930s. The new municipal building (above), which contained city hall as well as the police and fire departments, was completed in 1937 on the corner of Miner Street and Graceland Avenue, where the original library had just been razed. After a brief stay in the Des Plaines State Bank building, a new library (below) was added next door to city hall.

Rand Park (above) opened in 1940. The Des Plaines Park District purchased the Kufke farm in 1935, and with funding assistance from the WPA, built the recreational facility, which included a huge horseshoe-shaped swimming pool, baseball diamonds, tennis courts, and a field house. It also held concerts and carnivals. Today, the Mystic Waters water park is on the site and is operated by the park district. WPA funds also paid for the design of the post office (below). It opened in 1941 and was the post office headquarters until 1976.

UNITED STATES POST OFFICE
Des Plaines, Ill.

By the 1940s, downtown had really filled in. In addition to longtime shops like Spiegler's (above), several chain stores had moved in. On this stretch of Ellinwood Street, there was a Jewel and a Woolworths. Farther down at the intersection of Center Street, there were Ben Franklin and Walgreens stores. Along with the shops on Lee and Miner Streets, the stores made for an active, attractive shopping district.

Across the tracks, Brown's Department Store was at the corner of Pearson and Miner Streets. It was later replaced by a Sears store (below) and the building still stands today. Square Deal Shoes and Wahl's Jewelers are now located in the buildings to the left and both remain in business on Miner Street.

SCENE - DES PLAINES, ILL.

The above photograph looks at Ellinwood Street from the east. The park in the foreground ran along the railroad tracks, the depot is at the far right, and the Des Plaines State Bank building is in the distance. Residents loved to stroll around and enjoy the downtown shops and parks.

Des Plaines was growing rapidly in the 1920s and 1930s, with the population tripling between World War I and World War II, from about 3,000 residents to nearly 10,000. New homes were being built all over town, especially in the garden district. The Plew Homes company built many of the new houses.

SCENE NEW SUBDIVISION DES PLAINES ILL

The 1935 and 1938 floods hit the community hard. While longtime residents understood the river's frequent wrath, many newcomers were caught off guard. The photograph below shows River Road near Rand Road, with the Northwestern Hospital, the first hospital in Des Plaines, on the left. It began operating here in 1931 and continued until 1951. It was later converted into a motel, which still operates today.

Eventually there were three train lines crossing Des Plaines, all of which crisscrossed within several hundred yards of each other, creating a triangle called the Deval interchange. With the lines crossing in such close proximity, there was a need for a control tower. This spot has become a notable place for train enthusiasts.

In 1935, the Chicago & North Western Railroad introduced the Twin Cities 400 on its route from Chicago to St. Paul. The diesel engine was so named because it could traverse the 400 miles in 400 minutes. Soon the 400 and other diesel trains were used on other lines, including those serving Des Plaines, making faster commutes for residents. The steam engine era was officially over. (Photograph by Jeff Delhaye, taken at the Illinois Railway Museum.)

In 1941, Douglas Aircraft established its factory, airfield, and headquarters in Orchard Place. On 1,460 acres of what used to be farmland, they built runways and tested the Army's famed C-54 Skymaster. At the height of the war, 17,000 people were employed at the plant. Below, a Skymaster is on the assembly line in 1945. (Both, courtesy of the Chicago History Museum.)

A C-54 Skymaster is seen here in the air. In 1945, the B-29 *Enola Gay* (below), the plane that dropped the atomic bomb on Hiroshima and was named after pilot Paul Tibbitz's mother, made a visit to the Douglas Aircraft plant. After the war, the plant closed and Chicago opened O'Hare International Airport on the site in 1946. For a time, it was one of the busiest airports in the world. (Below, courtesy of Clifford Wesa.)

On February 1, 1945, these 27 employees of the DoALL Company and its subsidiary, Contour Saws, expressed their feelings towards the war. Their sign says, "Let's tie file bands to Hitler's pants, and keep him from getting back into France." The DoALL Company was formed by Leighton Wilkie to manufacture saws and drills in an old Des Plaines pickle factory. In 1942, DoALL became one of the first manufacturers in the area to employ women. (Courtesy of DoALL Company.)

Camp Pine was located along the Des Plaines River, in the forest preserves on the north end of town. It served as a German prisoner of war (POW) camp in World War II. Captured German soldiers were put to work on many area farms. Above, POW Rudolf Velte and another unidentified POW pose for a photograph with sugar beet farmer Eugene Carl, who is kneeling in the center with his dog Rex. After the war, Camp Pine (below) was used as a Girl Scout camp.

Most of the German soldiers were moved between different camps during the war. Above, POWs at Green Valley Farms pose for a photograph with farm owner Russell Mahler (kneeling in foreground), Fred Mahler (standing, third from left), and August Sell (center, raising his hand). Several Germans continued to correspond with the farm families they had worked with after the war. It was clear from their letters that they were treated better here than in other camps. POW Rudolph Velte is at left.

Six

POSTWAR TO MODERN DAY

After the war, there was a population explosion in Des Plaines. From around 10,000 residents during the war, the population grew to more than 28,000 by 1956. Where farmers once grew crops, developers now grew houses. (Courtesy of Alfini Construction Company.)

The Villas is a unique oval-shaped subdivision begun in the 1920s on local farmland. With the Great Depression halting construction, the development did not take off until later. These before and after photographs show the dramatic change in the landscape. The above image is an aerial view from before World War II with the Villas off in the distance. The aerial photograph below was taken during the population boom of the 1950s. (Above, courtesy of DoAll Company; below, courtesy of BorgWarner.)

Developers like Alfini Builders built tracts of houses on what had previously been farmland. While there was a serious need for new houses, there was less need for locally grown fruits, vegetables, and flowers. With greater air and road transportation, crops and flowers could be brought in from greater distances. Although these developments destroyed the farming and greenhouse industries in Des Plaines, residents adapted. (Both, courtesy of Alfini Construction Company.)

Ray Kroc opened the first franchised McDonald's in Des Plaines on April 15, 1955. Kroc was a blender salesman, and when he sold his Prince Castle Multi Mixer to the McDonald brothers for their restaurant in San Bernadino, California, he saw an opportunity. The Des Plaines restaurant was actually the ninth McDonald's restaurant, but it was the first one that was franchised, paving the way for rapid expansion. Kroc took over the McDonald's Corporation in 1961, and grew it into the largest fast food chain in the world. (Left, photograph used with permission from McDonald's Corporation; below, courtesy of Ken Bender.)

James Ballowe and his wife, Marilyn, opened the Choo Choo Restaurant (above) in 1951. Food is delivered to booths on model train cars that circle the diner, making it a popular destination for kids and train enthusiasts. It is still located on the corner where the bandstand used to be. One story says that Ray Kroc visited the Choo Choo when he was preparing to open his new McDonald's burger stand a few blocks down the street. He reassured the manager that his new restaurant posed no threat, as it was just a drive-in. Considering that both are still in business today, it appears he was right. (Above, courtesy of Stan Kotecki; below, courtesy of David Whittingham.)

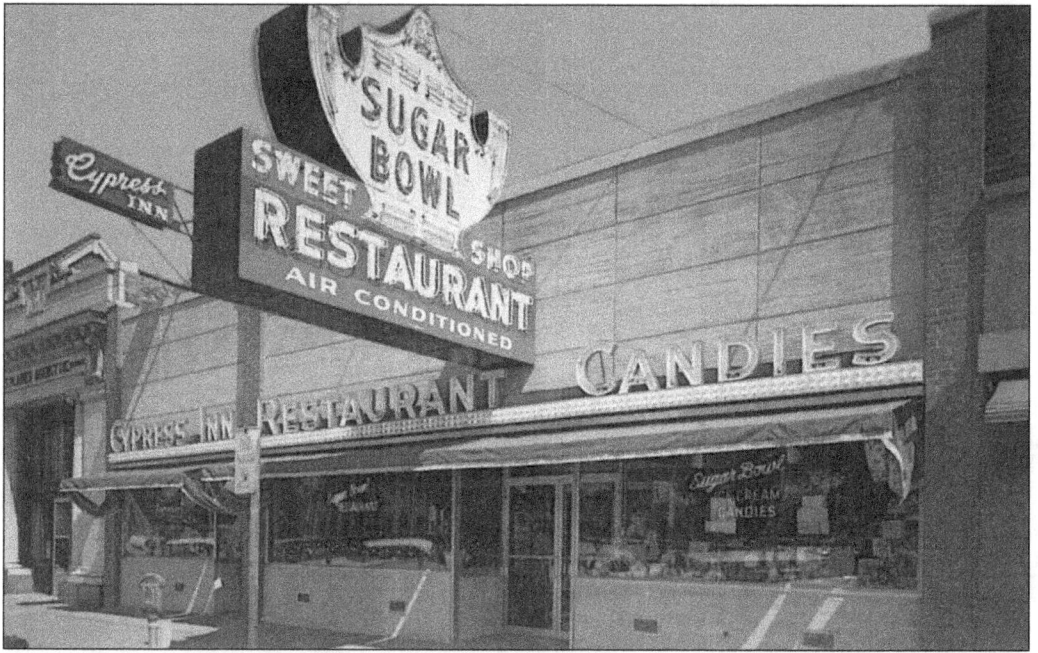

The Sugar Bowl today is a classic 1950s cafe with a classic marquee. The diner actually dates much farther back, originally opening in 1921. It was both a restaurant and candy shop that made its own candy. The back of this postcard reads, "Serving the best as always in snacks and complete meals. Try our own hand-made ice cream in package or at the fountain. Hand-rolled and hand-dipped chocolates made in our kitchens." In the note the sender says, "Love to eat here."

Runde's Dairy was a popular spot for an ice cream. It was located on Oakton Street and later became known as Bill's dairy. It was popular with families after Little League baseball games. As the population grew, Oakton Street developed into a business district as well.

Many kids caught their first fish at the Fisherman's Dude Ranch. John Redding and his wife, Maryanne, opened the ranch in 1956. It had a 14-acre spring-fed lake as well as five trout ponds. Visitors could catch bass, bluegills, catfish, trout, walleye, and even northern pike. Fishers paid for their catch by the pound and could even have the fish cleaned.

In the 1950s, several major highways were built through the Des Plaines area. Interstate 90 and the Tri-State Tollway created even faster transit between Chicago and the surrounding suburbs. To elevate the tollway, lakes were dug throughout the forest preserves. In the above image, two children stand on what used to be their farm, which was being excavated into a pit for a lake. Axehead Lake (below) is another one of these lakes and provides recreational opportunities to residents. The Tri-State Tollway is in the background. Other lakes in town include Belleau, Peterson, Big Bend, Beck, Mary Anne, Opeka, and Shagbark.

Lake Opeka and the surrounding Lake Park were created on the south side of town in the late 1950s. The 40-acre lake is popular with sailors and anglers. The park, which totals 60 acres, is run by the Des Plaines Park District. In addition to the lake, the park also features a golf course, playgrounds, and picnic areas. Below, Charles Pezoldt and Ferdinand C. Arndt of the Des Plaines Park District look over plans during the construction of Lake Park at Lake Opeka.

On October 25, 1960, John F. Kennedy made an appearance at the O'Hare Inn as he passed through Des Plaines on his presidential campaign. He spoke of taking his message of a responsible, progressive government to the Republican strongholds of the suburbs. Des Plaines Police sergeant Willard Blume directs traffic as Kennedy's motorcade passes by. (Photograph by Amasa "Pug" Kennicott, Des Plaines Police Department.)

The Des Plaines Public Library moved into a new location just south of the old one, at Graceland Avenue and Thacker Street, in 1958. Many residents still remember the Boy Scouts using shopping carts to move books from the old building to the new one.

In 1974 and 1975, Des Plaines built a brand new civic center on the site of the previous municipal building, at Miner Street and Graceland Avenue. It featured a state-of-the-art police station in addition to offices for city departments and the mayor. (Courtesy of the City of Des Plaines.)

In the 1970s, the city revamped downtown by building the Des Plaines Mall just south of the train depot. Spiegler's moved in and was one of the mall's anchor stores. The new Herbert H. Behrel Parking Plaza stood next to the train tracks on Ellinwood Street. Its distinctive circular ramp stood out, giving the entire business district a new look. Both the mall and parking garage were torn down between 1996 and 1998 so the city could create another new vision for downtown. (Above, courtesy of Peggy Wetter of Northwest Public Relations; below, courtesy of Michael Reher.)

Holy Family Hospital opened on June 12, 1961, and was run by the Sisters of the Holy Family of Nazareth. The hospital was recognized for its promotion of general health in the community as well as its effective management, keeping its room rates and patient charges among the lowest of all the area hospitals. Today, Holy Family is part of the Resurrection hospital system.

In 1974, Kinder Hardware celebrated its 100th anniversary. Already the longest running business in Des Plaines, it continued until 2006 as Kinder Industrial Supply, run by the descendants of Benjamin F. Kinder. (Photograph by Mary V. Wright.)

The famous Kinder House was moved just a few blocks in 1968 to its current home at the corner of Pearson Street and Prairie Avenue. It has since been restored and now serves as part of the Des Plaines History Center.

Located at the very busy intersection of River and Rand Roads, many recall the distinctive, eccentric, and very shiny Hub Cap Place. People joked that the business received the majority of its inventory as it rolled off of cars that took the turn onto River Road too fast. (Photograph by Dick & Mary Murray.)

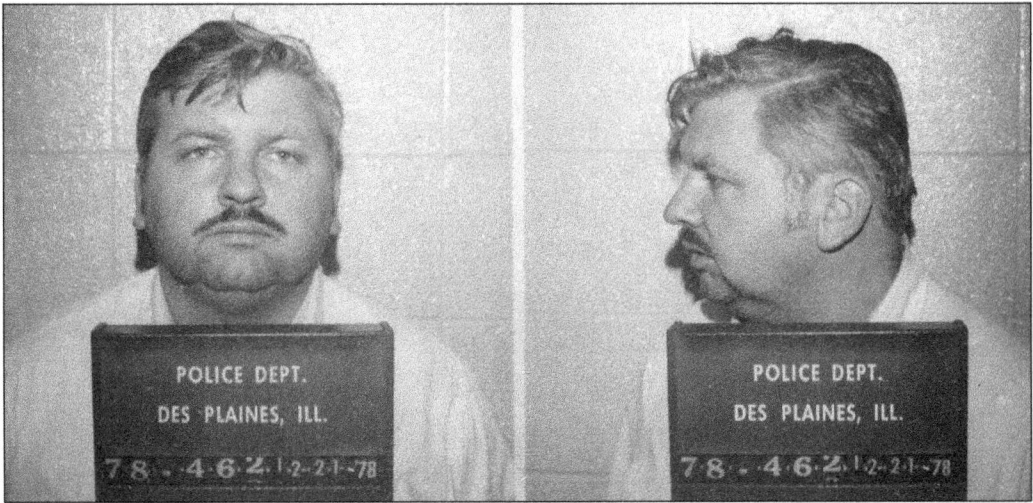

The Des Plaines Police Department is credited with cracking the case of serial killer John Wayne Gacy. Arrested on December 21, 1978, he was convicted of killing 33 young boys. He was sentenced to death and executed in May 1994. Gacy strangled most of his victims and many were buried in the crawl space beneath his Norwood Park home. The Des Plaines police were investigating the missing persons case of Robert Piest, who was last seen at the Nissen Pharmacy in Des Plaines. The police trailed Gacy and discovered the bodies under his house. Below are the Des Plaines police officers who worked on the case: Dave Hachmeister, Jim Kautz, Ron Robinson, Capt. Joseph Kozenczak, Walter Lang, Ron Adams, Ralph Tovar, Robert Schultz, James Pickell, Jim Ryan, and Mike Albrecht. (Both, courtesy of the Des Plaines Police Department.)

On May 25, 1979, American Airlines Flight 191 crashed shortly after takeoff. All 258 passengers and 13 crewmembers aboard the DC-10 were killed, as well as two people on the ground. At the time, it was the deadliest airline accident on American soil. The accident occurred after the left engine separated from the aircraft, which further damaged the left wing. It crashed in a field near a Des Plaines trailer community on the west side of town. The wreckage was still on fire when the emergency crews arrived. (Courtesy of Nathan Belonsky.)

All Saints Cemetery contains the gravesites of many famous people, including Olympian Annette Rogers, major league baseball players Lew Fonseca, Charles Leo "Gabby" Hartnett, and Fred C. Lindstrom, broadcaster Harry Caray, legendary DePaul University basketball coach Ray Meyer, NFL football players John "Paddy" Driscoll and George "Moose" Connor, opera singer and circus magnate Robert Edward Ringling, and many notable business executives and politicians. (Photograph by David Whittingham.)

In 1986, the Des Plaines River had its most destructive flood to date. On October 1, the river crested at 10.88 feet over flood stage, the highest crest ever recorded. The disaster caused more than $35 million in damage to more than 10,000 buildings and hundreds of businesses. (Above, courtesy of Peggy Wetter of Northwest Public Relations; below, courtesy of the Des Plaines Police Department.)

In 2000, as part of a downtown redevelopment plan, the Des Plaines Public Library reopened in an 80,000-square-foot facility on the previous site of the ill-fated Des Plaines Mall. The library is now a centerpiece of downtown Des Plaines, drawing thousands of visitors each month, who check out more than a million materials each year. (Photograph by David Whittingham.)

In 2011, Des Plaines was granted one of the few Illinois gaming licenses, and the 147,000-square-foot Rivers Casino opened. Being the closest Illinois casino to Chicago and being very close to O'Hare International Airport have helped it succeed. It is anticipated that it will bring in $150 million in tax revenue for Illinois and Des Plaines. (Photograph by David Whittingham.)

The Des Plaines History Center is on Pearson Street just south of Ellinwood Street. The center maintains the historic Kinder House on the corner and has a visitor center next door featuring extensive archives and rotating exhibits. The center hosts numerous programs promoting and celebrating local history.

Some things never change: in 2008, the Des Plaines River recorded its second worst flood, which crested at 10 feet over flood stage. Though not as severe as the 2008 flood, the river flooded again in 2010 and 2011. (Courtesy of Des Plaines Department of Public Works and Engineering.)

Visit us at
arcadiapublishing.com

www.ingramcontent.com/pod-product-compliance
Lightning Source LLC
Chambersburg PA
CBHW080619110426
42813CB00006B/1556